CLARITY IS POWER

Q & A

"Clarity is Power" book series, is a collection of wisdom from thought-provoking Q and A with renowned Mahatria. His unique gift of answering questions spontaneously is captured in this book, offering life-changing insights.

The "Clarity is Power" series comprises 11 illuminating volumes, each addressing essential aspects of life:

1. Attitudes
2. Self-Discipline
3. Emotional Development
4. Relationships
5. Marriage
6. Parenting
7. Student Life
8. Career Growth
9. Leadership and Entrepreneurship
10. Spirituality
11. Faith

Mahatria Spiritualist | Thought leader | Diviner of infinitheism

For nearly three decades, Mahatria has empowered millions worldwide to achieve holistic abundance. His profound wisdom uplifts people in health, wealth, love, bliss, and spirituality.

infinitheism, the path divined by Mahatria, inspires breakthroughs for anyone who ardently desires abundance by transforming the human spirit to have faith in its infinite potential.

First published in India

MANJUL

Manjul Publishing House

• 2nd Floor, Usha Preet Complex,
42 Malviya Nagar, Bhopal 462 003 - India
• C-16, Sector 3, Noida, Uttar Pradesh 201301 – India
Website: www.manjulindia.com

Distribution Centres:
Ahmedabad, Bengaluru, Bhopal, Kolkata, Chennai,
Hyderabad, Mumbai, New Delhi, Pune

In association with:

infinitheism

3, 3rd Cross Road, R A Puram,
Chennai, Tamil Nadu, India
www.infinitheism.com

CAREER GROWTH (CLARITY IS POWER)

by

mahātria Rā

This edition first published in 2016
Third impression 2024

ISBN 978-93-5543-433-3

Printed and bound in India by Thomson Press (India) Ltd.

CLARITY IS POWER

Q & A

CAREER GROWTH

mahātria

CONTENTS

1	May I know what efforts I should take to become an empowering communicator?	6
2	I am working as a middle-level manager. I treat people as my friends. So I am very flexible with them. I am not able to deliver my 100% at work. Please help.	10
3	I expect punctuality from everybody in my organisation, which is not happening. I am totally upset. Of late, I take out my anger on people who report to me.	14
4	How do you manage people with criminal intent at workplace? Sometimes we find this even in institutions...	16
5	Should I work for rewards and awards or should I work for satisfaction? What should be my focus?	20
6	I work for an MNC as Head - Back-end operations. I have been promoted recently to handle both front-end and back-end operations at present. While a promotion like this should make me feel ecstatic, I am feeling very nervous. Why?	22
7	What do you do if you get a bad boss?	26
8	Don't you think Corporate India is squeezing too much juice out of people? Should so much work be extracted out of individuals?	30

CONTENTS

9 From a salesman's perspective, what is the difference between 'Price', 'Cost' and 'Value'? 34

10 It has been my desire from the age of 20 to reach the top position in an organisation. However, I have not grown out of my comfort zone in my career spanning 16-years. I want to achieve what I have never achieved before. 40

11 I have recently taken up marketing as my career. Can you give me some tips to develop my negotiation skills? 44

12 I tend to develop cold feet when working under pressure. Teach me how to work efficiently under pressure. 50

13 After I got an award from my management, I feel it has gone into my head and I have not been performing well in my duties at office and not living up to my potential. Please help me overcome the barrier. 54

14 Knowledge is to be shared. Whenever a person close to me makes a mistake, I teach him how to respond in a particular situation. But people always get me wrong mistaking it for arrogance. What should I do? 56

15 I have received my first offer letter from one of the premium organisations. This also means relocation to a new city, leaving parents and comforts... What should I do? 60

1

May I know what efforts I should take to become an empowering communicator?

The power of a person is the power of their voice. The power of their voice is expressed through the power of their communication.

But then all of us are not necessarily communicators. There is a lot of difference between talking and communicating. Talking is like scribbling whereas communication is like writing. While talking can be purposeless, communication has to serve a purpose.

What happens in a class when two students talk? They get punished. Whereas when a student knows how to communicate, they become a class leader.

Good communication has three attributes.

1. What to say - Content
2. How to say - Emotions
3. When to say - Timing

'What to say?' is 'mind to mind' communication. My communication conveys my thoughts to you. What to say is the content of my communication and it has to be very clear.

'How to say?' is all about emotions. It is 'heart to heart' communication. Emotions, which you add to your communication makes your communication an empowering one because now it has emotional appeal.

'When to say?' is all about timing. The right message in the right manner in the right time will give you the right results.

To ensure your communication is empowering, follow a few simple steps. Primarily, there has to be poise in your action. There has to be grace in the body language so that people don't deviate from the topic and their concentration is not diverted.

Secondly, always take the centre stage. People, who operate from the centre stage, whether it is a training session or a board meeting or in a group discussion, always enjoy a psychological advantage.

Thirdly, remember, leadership begins with eyes. Eyes are very powerful. You can communicate so many things through your eyes. When I look into the eyes of the audience I take my audience along with me. They stay connected with me.

And finally, don't talk with some object in your hand. Leave your hands free and it will enhance your non-verbal communication.

Technology can give you information. Communication alone can bring about the transformation. Nothing is more powerful than the power of human voice. ●

Talking is like scribbling whereas communication is like writing.

While talking can be purposeless, communication has to serve a purpose.

mahatria

2

I am working as a middle-level manager. I treat people as my friends. So I am very flexible with them. I am not able to deliver my 100% at work. Please help.

It doesn't mean just because the pawn, the queen and the king come from the same box they share equal significance on the chessboard. The king is the king and the pawn is only a pawn on the board. By choosing to be a good friend to your colleagues, outside the office, you show yourself and the world that you are a wonderful human being. If you do the same thing inside the office then that would make you a lousy manager.

Every role has some primary responsibilities. How much ever we do in other aspects if we fail to live up to the primary responsibility of a role, then we have let the role down. It is not about whether the driver is nice to you or not - his primary responsibility is to drive the vehicle safely. Will you excuse him if he is very nice to you, always smiling but dents the car twice a week?

As parents, if we provide everything materialistic to our children, but fail to guide them morally, then we are a failure in parenting. So it is with a manager. Getting the job done by managing the resources is the primary responsibility of a manager and no compromise is allowed. The same colleagues with whom you are not able to deliver the 100% will not tell you tomorrow,

"Thank you for being such a good friend," but will ask you, "Why were you not a good enough manager?"

We teach children, 'Work while you work and play while you play'. Manage while you are a manager and befriend where you will have to be a friend. In all roles of your life, first fulfill your primary responsibility and only then extend yourself into the secondary responsibilities.

First succeed as a manager inside the office. Post-working hours reach out to them as a friend.

Good managers always have an iron fist in a velvet glove. ●

Every role has some primary responsibilities. How much ever we do in other aspects, if we fail to live up to the primary responsibility of a role, then we have let the role down.

mahātria

3

I expect punctuality from everybody in my organisation, which is not happening.
I am totally upset. Of late, I take out my anger on people who report to me.

Transformation of actions can be instantaneous, but transformation of character takes time. To achieve character change even in one individual takes time, but here you are attempting to achieve a collective transformation. It takes time, but it can be achieved. You need to show a lot of character to achieve this character change in others.

Anger can only change the actions of a person, and these changes are always temporary. Persistent communication will change the thinking of a person, and that change can be permanent. So, keep explaining the value of time, the value of punctuality, the value of discipline. And remember, the time to correct a mistake is never during the mistake. You will only get self-justification in return. Education is best delivered when people are not expecting it. The sculptor never knows after which strike the stone will chip off, but it will eventually. Which sentence of yours would strike that transformation no one knows; but it will, eventually.

How do you manage people with criminal intent at workplace? Sometimes we find this even in institutions...

If meritorious performance is not the fundamental eligibility for recognition or promotion, sooner than later, the criminal intent will arise. In an environment where the only way one can look tall is by cutting somebody else's leg and making the other look short, criminal intent will grow. It's an inadequacy in the system. Under those circumstances, it is how you know to move your coins much more than sincerity, dedication, commitment and performance.

I remember talking to somebody from Corporate India a few weeks ago. He said that it is a disadvantage today to be super-efficient! He achieves his targets and leaves office by 6:30 p.m. to enjoy a balanced family life. A few of his colleagues, who are not focused during work hours, stretch themselves at the end of the day beyond 8:30 p.m., to complete their regular work. In the eyes of his boss, if the long hours are perceived as sincerity, then everybody will start thinking how to drag themselves beyond the office hours and score brownie points with the boss. This is a weakness of the system which develops the criminal intent.

When the rest of the classmates see that the one who is closest to the class teacher has become the class leader without any selection criteria, then every student in the class will think of ways to become close to the class teacher and will not strive to develop leadership qualities. Such inadequacies do exist in the system.

I would look at it this way! Here is a brilliant opportunity to be utilized by anyone who wants to grow in maturity, to differentiate the good from the bad, the right from the wrong, and people, who sweet-talk in your presence and bad-mouth behind you; for maturity is rarely gained in a perfect environment. Prudence, maturity and exposure are always developed in an imperfect environment; so see an imperfect work environment as an opportunity for you to develop your maturity.

Also, when you become the boss, strive to modify the system so that promotions and recognitions are given based on measurable meritorious performance and not on the perception which could be wrong. Let your team not suffer what you are going through. Let not others go through the deprivation that you have gone through. This will reduce the criminal intent in the work environment. ●

Prudence, maturity and exposure
are always developed in an
imperfect environment;
so see an imperfect work environment
as an opportunity for you
to develop your maturity.

mahātria

Should I work for rewards and awards or should I work for satisfaction? What should be my focus?

It is a true story that Dave Anderson and Jim Murphy joined American Railways on the same day. Twenty years later, Dave was still doing the same job but Jim became the Chairman of American Railways. Dave said, "I came to work for $1.75 an hour; Jim came to work for American Railways. That made all the difference."

Work is our only salvation. Work is the only way to progress. Nothing develops a person like work does. Work must be the primary form of worship. What you get by achieving your goal is insignificant compared to what you become in achieving your goal. It is not about rewards or awards or satisfaction. They are mere by-products for a person who discovers themselves through work. Happiness is the by-product of doing the work that gives you your inner expression. Success is the by-product of the world recognising the value you add through your work. And, when your work and results of your work become useful to the world, the by-product is that you discover the purpose of your life. ●

6

I work for an MNC as Head - Back-end operations. I have been promoted recently to handle both front-end and back-end operations at present. While a promotion like this should make me feel ecstatic, I am feeling very nervous. Why?

There are two kinds of fears. One is 'fear of facing something' and the other is 'fear of excellence'. The first one is negative, whereas the latter is positive. It is 'fear of facing something' that pushes people into inertia. It even keeps them from getting started. It kills their initiative and turns them into escapists. They live and die within their own shrunken comfort zones. It is evident that what you are going through doesn't fit into this category; for if that were the case, you wouldn't have reached where you've reached in life.

What you are going through is 'fear of excellence', which is a positive fear. You have professionally excelled in your earlier responsibility. The new chair is demanding new skills from you, which you aren't sure you have as yet. There is a sense of incompetence. In fact, a good corporate promotion is one where the person promoted feels a little incompetent in the new chair. This would make them expand their competence and the organisation too would expand in the process. The nervousness of Virat Kohli isn't about whether he can face Shaheen Afridi, but whether he can score another hundred. This is a positive fear. It is this fear - 'the fear of excellence' - that creates a world of competence; if not for this, we would be living in a world of compromise. It is actually 'desire for excellence' that is dressed as 'fear of excellence'.

During such circumstances, you should believe in your management. No management in today's competitive world will give you a responsibility unless they are convinced that you are capable of handling it. Have faith in the decision of your management - they've decided that you are good enough; that's why this promotion.

As a rule, when you don't have enough faith in yourself, have faith in those who have faith in you. Remember, courage is not the absence of fear, but the ability to go ahead in spite of fear. Go ahead and discover yourself. Trust me, very soon you will qualify yourself for the next promotion and embrace yet another level of 'fear of excellence'. You are on the right track. ●

A good corporate promotion is one, where the person promoted feels a little incompetent in the new chair. This would make them expand their competence and the organisation too would expand in the process.

mahātria

What do you do if you get a bad boss?

First remember, 'bad boss' is a perception and all perceptions are relative and subjective. A 'bad boss' just means that the chemistry between you and your boss isn't working, and it may be working perfectly with someone else.

Secondly, tell yourself, "I know what it feels like to work for a bad boss," and resolve to be a good boss when you become a boss. Don't do to others what you don't want to be done to you. Take this as your training ground to build your 'What not to do' qualities of a professional. See this as your training and learning ground.

Every professional who has hit the top, at some point of their career would have served an 'Oh no' boss.

In fact, 'bad' is the best training ground for 'good'. Failures teach you some of the best lessons in life, which success cannot.

Strength of character is developed by the obstacles you overcome. Tough times mould the personality of a person.

Actually tough students mould good teachers into great teachers. Wars provided the context to develop great technology. The cross became the symbol of Christianity and the *Kurukshetra* gave the world the *Bhagavad Gita*. Compressed coal becomes diamond. Bad always brings along good.

A bad boss can be the context for you to become an outstanding professional.

Of course, it's needless to remind present-day professionals - if need be, a few lines on a paper and a signature will give you a new boss. ●

*Failures teach you
some of the best lessons in life,
which success cannot.*

*Strength of character is developed
by the obstacles you overcome.*

*Tough times mould
the personality of a person.*

mahātria

8

Don't you think Corporate India is squeezing too much juice out of people? Should so much work be extracted out of individuals?

There are 365 days in a year. If you deduct 52 Sundays and 12 holidays, it leaves 301 days for work. Deduct 12 days of casual leave, 12 days of sick leave and 12 days of privilege leave. It leaves us with 265 days. Since we spend at least 12 hours away from work that accounts for 132 days (265 x 12 / 24). That leaves us with 133 days. We spend at least 2 hours at the workplace with coffee, social media, lunch and chatting with other colleagues which accounts for another 22 days (265 x 2 / 24). It leaves us with 111 days available for work. i.e., we invest just 30% of a year in work.

Of course, those of you with 5-day-weeks, those who do personal work during the work hours, those of you who keep searching for another job during your work hours, those of you on the net accessing personal mails, web surfing on favourite holiday destinations and e-chatting, those of you who counsel your colleagues, etc... has to calculate further down from the estimated 111 days.

Let us understand and get our perception about the sanctity of work right. You don't work for anybody. You work for yourself. Others may benefit from the effects of your work, but the main beneficiary of your work is yourself. You discover yourself through work. Work should be a happening and not a doing. Work should expand your personality. Work shouldn't be an effort, but it should be a flow. Work should be a celebration. You must dance your way to work and come back whistling your favourite tune.

The duration of work, the compensation package, the position at work - should all be details compared to the potential within you getting manifested through work. While at work you should not be aware of your time. Your work should not be quantified by what you are getting paid. If every homemaker begins to equate their work with the compensation they get, then this world will come to a grinding halt. You must always deliver more than what is expected of you. Give the best you can and be the best in whatever you do.

The food we eat, the clothes we wear, the roof above our head and the luxuries we enjoy are all the rewards we get from the work we do. Let your heart be ever filled with gratitude for the work you do. Work not only gives you the rewards of life, but it also adds a sense of purpose to life. So go to work with the same reverence and devotion with which you will visit a place of worship. This world will worship those who worship their work.

Let the effects of the work we do be the signature we leave behind in this world. ●

“

This world will worship those who worship their work.

mahātria

9

From a salesman's perspective, what is the difference between 'Price', 'Cost' and 'Value'?

The flat you bought could have carried a price of forty lakh rupees but the cost would get distributed across the period you possess it. It is difficult to assign a value for owning a house especially knowing the aspirations of every Indian in this regard. The freedom of being a house-owner, the confidence of having an asset and the status that it adds... remember, value is not what you pay for it but what it can do for you.

Price: The first thing most inexperienced salesmen do is, in their anxiety to close the sale, offer discounts. Selling by offering discounts is not smart selling. Every rupee of discount offered is loss of profit margins. For every rupee of profit lost, a proportionate turnover has to be generated to make up for what has been lost. A good salesman should not only sell but should sell with enough profit margins.

Breaking down the price into affordable sizes will help the buyer understand that it is affordable. It is in the finance company's ability to make every potential buyer believe that they can afford those monthly installments which has developed the consumer industry. Most buyers just pull in a string by stating that your price is too high. The other possibility is that the buyer may ask for a specific discount. Now only communicate and discuss the difference amount that is in contention and not the whole price. If you market only quality products and can also explain the quality benefits to the buyer, he may not mind buying, even if he has to create a budget for it.

Cost: Cost is spread over the entire period for which you use the product or service. Cost includes all future maintenance/repairs expenses too. If the product is maintenance-free and may not fail for the next five years, then the price and cost will be the same for the next five years. The value of the product is not what you pay for it, but what it can do for you. Cost negotiation involves a lot of education to be provided to the buyer, especially about the quality. Educate them on how the cost will increase, if they go for a product of lesser quality. Make them quality conscious.

Value: A prospect will buy from you when they want your product or service more than the money it costs. The undercurrent of the entire sales presentation is to build a value for your products in the prospect's mind. 'The value of the product depends on what the product can do for them and not what they have to pay for it'.

At the start of your presentation, in the prospect's mind, the value of Rs.100/- is 100 and the value of your product is zero. With every new benefit that you present to the prospect and get them to acknowledge it, the value of the product goes up, while the value of Rs.100/- remains 100. So it is very important that you never ask for the order too early - not till you have established the value of your product else it will ring an alarm in the mind of the prospect that you are more interested in the sale than offering them a solution.

Never ask for the order unless you had qualified the buying signals of the prospect with enough 'Trial closes'. Trial close is posing a question to the prospect like, "Is it within the budget or you need to take a sanction?", "Are you paying by credit card or cheque?", "Would you want the delivery immediately or on an auspicious day?"

In all these trial close questions, though you are not asking for the order, you are providing the prospect with alternatives to choose from. Which ever of these options they choose from, you know they are providing you with enough buying signals. After qualifying the prospect with a few trial closes to convince yourself of those buying signals, then you can ask for the order.

However, to the trial close question that you posed to the prospect, instead of choosing one of the alternatives you have provided them with, if the prospect goes on the defensive and says something negative, then you know that there are no buying signals. Whenever a prospect says 'No' to your product, please understand that you cannot get them to change their decision. Provide some additional information or value addition about your product which will enable them to make a new decision.

Play this psychological warfare fairly and create a 'win-win' situation for both, the buyer and yourself.

A prospect will buy from you
when they want
your product or service
more than the money it costs.
The undercurrent of the
entire sales presentation
is to build a value for your products
in the prospect's mind.

mahātria

10

It has been my desire from the age of 20 to reach the top position in an organisation. However, I have not grown out of my comfort zone in my career spanning 16-years. I want to achieve what I have never achieved before.

Our comfort zones become our prison, within which our potential stays locked up. A seed is very well protected as long as it remains a seed. There is security in remaining a seed; whereas a plant is always vulnerable. To sprout into a plant makes the seed susceptible, but what is the purpose of a seed? It contains a thousand forests within, and it is in the transcendence of the seed into a plant that these possibilities unfold. If the seed remains transfixed as the kernel, it is no better than a pebble on the beach.

Either transcend your comfort zone and reach the higher planes of life, or stay transfixed within your comfort zone and remain stagnant. Don't be afraid to give up certainty for uncertainty. It is astounding how the world makes way for a resolute soul and how obstacles move out of the path of a man who is determined to make it in life.

There is no more risk in 'change'. In fact, 'not to change' is actually risky because it leaves you where you are. When there is no security TO life itself, where is the question of security IN life? After all, what is growth? Growth is giving up who you are to become what you can be. That which does not change, does not grow. That which does not grow, dies.

Challenges and hiccups are bound to be there on the path of an achiever. Freedom comes not from escaping them, but in transcending them. Throw yourself into the unknown. Do what you have never done before. Do what you thought you cannot. Make a daring move. Take a rebellious plunge.

If people who walked this planet before us had chosen to stay transfixed to their comfort zones, then we would have nothing of what we have right now. All inventions and discoveries have come from people who ventured bravely into the unknown. The next rung of the ladder is always an unknown factor. The next moment of life has its uncertainties. Death alone is certain; life can never be. Seek the unknown and make it known. However tough the consequences may be, face it. Keep expanding your comfort zone and thus expand your life.

Self-depreciation is a crime. Do not become your own restraint. Be sure that your success will never rise above the boundaries of your comfort zone. You have to break open the walls of your comfort zone. There is no turning point within the comfort zone. All turning points in life are beyond the periphery of your comfort zones. Confidence grows only when you do things that you have never done before and do things that you thought you cannot. Self-belief is born when you transcend your comfort zone. Transcend your comfort zone and turn your life around. ●

That which does not change, does not grow.

That which does not grow, dies.

mahātria

11

I have recently taken up marketing as my career. Can you give me some tips to develop my negotiation skills?

Selling is a sort of psychological warfare in which both the buyer and the seller are trying to empower the other for a personal advantage. The mindset of a salesperson for a negotiation is more important than their negotiating skills. Selling is transference of thoughts and feelings. So, every time before you start a negotiation, remind yourself of the following:

1. Refuse to quit. Tell yourself - as long as I don't quit, I don't fail. Never quit in your mind. Keep reminding yourself that even if all the doors seem shut by the competition, a re-entry is still possible. There must definitely be a way in. Let me reiterate that as long as you haven't quit, you haven't failed.

2. Do not take any refusal from the prospect too personally. Understand that all rejections are professional rejections. They are refusing the product and rejecting the salesperson in you, not 'you the person'. When a prospect rejects your business proposition, it doesn't mean they are rejecting you.

3. Do not carry any negative thoughts or feelings about your product. For example, if you feel that your product is actually very expensive, that's exactly what you'll transfer to your prospect subliminally. Program yourself with the right thoughts and feelings about the product you are selling.

4. Develop an intense 'desire to gain'. During negotiations 'fear of loss' binds both the potential buyer and the salesman. Load yourself with enough positive affirmations like 'I am walking away with this order', 'this case is mine', 'today is my day', 'I'll clinch a deal that's fair to both the prospect and my organisation', 'I shall go back to my office with pride', 'I want the order today and I want it now'. Let the positive feelings in you empower the defensive prospect.

5. Right through the negotiation, respond; do not react. Irrespective of how the prospect provokes you, no matter how unfavourable the situation is, even if the case seems to be slipping, do not react. Reactions make you desperate. They cloud your intelligence and make you lose your capacity to think. Never get provoked. Do not become a victim of circumstance. Choose your response. Carry clarity in your mind, tranquillity in your heart and a smile on your face. Do what you want to do, and not what you are provoked to do.

6. Never become part of the prospect's problem. As long as you stay emotionally detached from the prospect's problem, you can be a solution to them and help them to overcome their problem.

7. Throughout a negotiation, speak only of virtues. People like it and it motivates them to be good, at least with you. Be good and you will magnetise more good.

8. Right through the negotiation, listen to your prospect through your eyes, not just through your ears. Keep looking into the eyes of the prospect. Eyes are much more empowering than the voice.

9. Let your negotiation be driven by personal values and organisational policies. Rather than letting your moods and desperation guide you during a negotiation, allow your personal values and professional policies to govern the negotiation. This will build consistency into your approach. This will help you from giving in to a bad deal. This will prevent you from being outsmarted by your prospect. Stand by your values and policies.

10. Do everything in your capacity to create an impression in the prospect's mind that they will neither lose money nor face by buying from you. (Here I make an assumption that you are selling a genuine product that will be of help to the prospect). Also let them understand that if they don't buy from you, they would stand to lose the benefits that your product can offer them.

The right mindset during a negotiation will certainly improve the closing percentage of every salesperson. Even if you are an extraordinary salesperson, remember to clean your slate and paint a picture of positive thoughts, conducive to a smart negotiation.

If you have to improve your status in life, then you have to improve your performance. Good performance is a product of the right mindset. Have the mindset of a champion... a champion salesperson.

“

If you have to improve your status in life, then you have to improve your performance.

Good performance is a product of the right mindset.

mahātria

I tend to develop cold feet when working under pressure. Teach me how to work efficiently under pressure.

At every stage of your life, there will be challenges and issues. At the time of birth from the cozy womb you had to fight your way to be born. Learning to suckle was the next challenge for you. From making sounds to communicating was a challenge for you; from scribbling to handwriting was a challenge. At every stage you are promoted, and promotion is just a confirmation that the next level of challenges is going to be placed before you.

If you want to be a world champion, you have to be better than everybody; otherwise you are not a world champion. When you win in semi-finals, it means that you have upgraded yourself to the next level of challenge. Every issue solved, every problem managed, every question answered just promotes you to face the challenge at the next level.

In the context of the new challenge, the previous challenge which you have overcome appears easy. So psychologically there is an inherent tendency in every human being to face challenges one level below than where they are right now; but that is not called growth! One level ahead from where you are is called promotion and one level below is called demotion.

Your maturity levels are always one leg below the experiences you are encountering in life. This very experience has been designed for you to gain this maturity. So it's only in facing situations bigger than you, you are going to gain the maturity. It is time for you to reveal unto yourself and to the world what you are capable of. So, face the challenge, even if it is bigger than you at this point in time.

Learn to grow out of challenges. Get a kick out of it! Ask yourself 'What is the issue today through which I can grow... what is the challenge that I am going to face right now, which will take me to the next level of maturity in life... what is the next tough, pressurising, difficult, challenging exam that I will pass, and when I pass that will be my promotion'.

Life is a series of challenges designed to create you. The caterpillar wanted to develop its wings so much that it went into the cocoon to develop its wings. It's the pressure of the cocoon that creates the context for a caterpillar to develop the wings. If that pressure is not there, caterpillar cannot develop the wings. A human being gets created under pressure. Go through it. It will be a revelation to you at the end. ●

“

It is time for you to reveal unto yourself and to the world what you are capable of. So, face the challenge, even if it is bigger than you at this point in time.

mahātria

After I got an award from my management, I feel it has gone into my head and I have not been performing well in my duties at office and not living up to my potential. Please help me overcome the barrier.

Success should feed your sense of responsibility and not your ego. Awards are mere milestones. They are not the destination. More people in the world have perished unable to handle their success, than not knowing how to handle their failures.

Getting promoted in 4th standard or for that matter even coming first in the class in your 4th standard means nothing to you in 5th standard. Once you step down from the winning podium, you are only a defending champion. Your results of the previous game give you no advantage in the next game.

Yesterday's success doesn't deserve today's applause. After every success, every award, let the lingering questions be, "What next? What more?" This will create futuristic thinking in you, which will in turn design your future. Stop looking back. Start looking ahead. Raise the bar. Set a new goal. Move on... ●

14

Knowledge is to be shared. Whenever a person close to me makes a mistake, I teach him how to respond in a particular situation. But people always get me wrong mistaking it for arrogance. What should I do?

Firstly, you cannot teach those who cannot see a teacher in you. Secondly, though feedback is given to improve a person, they often perceive it as 'you are pointing at their mistakes'. The intention behind the feedback is to tell the person 'where they can become better'; but they perceive it as you telling them 'where they were wrong'. Thirdly, most of the communication gaps occur because we communicate to an unprepared mind. To illustrate my point, let me share this story:

A man from a village, with his innocence still intact, came to a city. With pangs of hunger he visited a roadside eatery. He asked the bearer, “What can you give me that will satiate my hunger?” “Vada is good,” was the reply. “What is the cost of vada that would satisfy my hunger?” questioned the hungry soul. Prompt came the reply, “Five rupees.” The villager enquired, “Are you telling me that vada will satisfy my hunger and it will cost me five rupees?” A little irritated, the bearer asked in return, “Do you want the vada or not?” The man ordered for the vada, consumed the first and he was still hungry. So he went for the second, but was still hungry. Then went in the third, fourth, fifth, and also the sixth - the stomach seemed to be a bottomless pit. He was still hungry. Finally, the seventh did the job. His hunger was satiated.

The innocent villager judiciously picked up a five-rupee coin and extended it to the bearer. To his utter shock, the bearer demanded thirty-five rupees, and clarified, "You had seven vadas." The villager shot back, "I clearly asked you, 'What is the cost of the vada that would satisfy my hunger?' and you said 'five rupees'. Only the seventh satisfied my hunger and the other six did not fulfil the purpose. So I will pay only for the seventh and not for the other six."

If the six did not precede the seventh *vada*, it couldn't have made the difference. If only six *vadas* had gone in, still it wouldn't have made the difference. The six *vadas* refer to the communication that is required to prepare the mind of the receiver to receive your advice. The seventh *vada* is the advice. If you learn the art of communicating to a prepared mind, you make a difference to people close to you, and also you will not be perceived as arrogant.

Having said all this, I wish to tell you, if your intentions are genuine, and the motive is only to make a difference, go ahead and do it, even at the risk of the world misunderstanding you.

I wish to share with you an adapted version of 'The Paradoxical Commandments' by Dr. Kent M. Keith that were written on the wall of Mother Teresa's home for children in Kolkata.

'People are often unreasonable, irrational, and self-centered. Forgive them anyway.

If you are kind, people may accuse you of selfish, ulterior motives. Be kind anyway.

If you are successful, you will win some unfaithful friends and some genuine enemies. Succeed anyway.

If you are honest and sincere, people may deceive you. Be honest and sincere anyway.

What you spend years creating, others could destroy overnight. Create anyway.

If you find serenity and happiness, some may be jealous. Be happy anyway.

The good you do today, will often be forgotten. Do good anyway.

Give the best you have, and it will never be enough. Give your best anyway.

In the final analysis, it is between you and God. It was never between you and them anyway'.

I have received my first offer letter from one of the premium organisations. This also means relocation to a new city, leaving parents and comforts... What should I do?

First job, first employer, first boss and first salary... Every 'first' related to your career isn't something you are going to forget in a lifetime. In fact, all career progresses will be benchmarked against these firsts. Your first organisation and your first job can have a major bearing on your work ethics all through your life.

Transition is never easy but without transition there is no evolution. There is no growth within your comfort zone. Unless you are willing to challenge yourself beyond your comfort zones, you cannot become what you can become. Sometimes, you need to 'give up' to 'go up'.

The law of life is 'When the lower is pushed, the higher delights'. When the body is pushed beyond its perceived limits, the mind delights. When the body tells you 'I can't walk one more block. I can't run another lap. I cannot trek anymore', and then when it is pushed beyond its perceived limits and it walks that additional block, runs another lap and treks further - the mind delights. Against the pleading of your body when you do a few more push-ups or a few more reps of the bicep curls or another dozen squats - the mind delights. When the lower - the body is pushed, the higher - the mind delights.

Likewise, quietening the mind is a struggle for the mind, but a delight to the intellect. So, whenever you try to do any process to develop your concentration, try to curtail the wandering nature of the mind and get it to focus on a single-point - the mind feels pushed but the higher - the intellect, delights. That's why clarity is always the fruit of concentration.

There is always this inner intellectual conflict between our instincts and conscience. Our instincts ask us to follow the path of 'pain and pleasure' while our conscience demands us to follow the path of 'right and wrong'. It is this that causes the intellectual split in us. What we call as guilt is nothing but the disapproval of the 'knower' in us to an act of the 'doer' in us; that is when the conscience doesn't endorse the instincts. Resolving this split and living as an integrated person is the struggle of the intelligence, but it is the delight of the higher - emotional personality. And so it is at every level. To be caught in the turbulence of various emotions is the natural way of an emotional being. To resolve these emotional turbulences and to be able to live in a state of emotional equanimity is the delight of the higher - the spiritual personality in us. That's why spiritual centeredness is achieved only when a person achieves purity in their feelings.

With all the examples and explanations, I am trying to drive only one point, 'When the lower is pushed, the higher delights'.

If you want an edge over the rest, then you need 'Horizontal Exposure with Vertical Expertise'. Think of anyone you look up to, be it in sports or industry or politics or cinema or even within the family - those who have an edge have it because of 'Horizontal Exposure with Vertical Expertise'. I won't ask you to settle down anywhere other than a place of your choice. I respect your feelings for your parents and friends. In fact, I am proud of you for that. But for sheer exposure, I think you should relocate yourself geographically for some time. So much of your personality will be shaped in the process.

Struggle, suffering, challenges, testing periods, tough times - in fact, all these are part of the vocabulary of a person who is seeing only the lower being pushed without recognising how the higher delights in the process. You are saying the caterpillar is being pushed. I am saying the butterfly is being born. Every time a human being is pushed, God delights... for, it is through this push that a human being is created. Align yourself to this spiritual truth and a lot about your life will change. ●

Unless you are willing to
challenge yourself
beyond your comfort zones,
you cannot become
what you can become.

mahātria